The Ferocious Silence

Darryl Price

Manufactured in the United States of America
First Edition

www.unknoweverything.com

All poems first presented in their most original forms to the Fictionaut online writer's community between 2014-2015. Grateful acknowledgement is made to the following spaces where some of these poems were first given permission to exist:

"I Want to Sing to You" was first published in Poetry Pacific., Winter 2015.
"Like A Pop-song, This is the Head of a Sunflower" was first published in Metazen.
"How To Remember Important Things" was first published in The Miscreant
"Weeds of the World(Unite!) was first published in Five Pure Slush Vol. 10. January 2016
"The Moon Rose Up on Its Tin Foil Bed" was first published in Leopardskin & Limes
"Our Love is Enough" was first published in the Olentangy Review
"The Sky Here's Full Stopped" was first published in Istanbul Literary Review #18

for Charlotte and Mel, as always

"We should insist on joy in spite of everything."
—Tom Robbins

Contents

How to Remember Important Things

Save the whales. Save the dolphins.
Save the bored housewives.
Save my hands, so often cupped over the sorrow in
being alive. Save the beautiful
made-up cherries of delight
I feel everywhere in your presence. Save the sprawling
landscapes
of late night cafeterias of the mind. Save the often
forgotten radios of our flying dreams. Save the hand-
printed love

letters of early morning light. Save the inexhaustible
curiosity of
a small interior poem of silence.
Save the naked air.
Save the Spanish tongue of Neruda.
Save the sparkle in
the brushstrokes of a Picasso.
Save storm and the rainbow.

Save the North Sea. Save shadows.
Save all hearts from
beginning to break again.
Save the ripped apart sky from
the rain of so many angry bombs leaking inside. Save the
secret handshake. Save the Pandas.
Save the sea turtles.
Save the roses. Save the last dance. Save the sailing boats
and floating planes of melting romance. Save whatever
makes

no sense. Save this feeling. Save the butterflies with
passionate, provocative kisses.
Save the question of imagination. Save the end
of the poem until you really need it. Save the
world from itself. Save your wild goodbyes. Save every
word.

With Nothing Here
But Me I Begin

to unwind looking for the answer.
I confess I wasn't so discreet
as life demanded, laughing like a
nowhere poet. Nothing relieved the
god awful boredom. Many times I
confess I hadn't really taken
the vitamins, crying like a court
jester thrown into a dungeon on
market day, and felt ashamed of all
human hypocrisy everywhere.
Many times over I confess I'm
paranoid; I can try to love the
police but they all act like Hitler
to me. Many times I confess there's
a sadness inside. Often I say
to myself I guess I can describe
a circle as well as the next guy.
I put forth my arms, look, I confess
to embrace the whole world, too, but just
because you're in it. Many times I

confess I've been places and seen things
that didn't appeal to me, weird things
worried me, like proselytizing guys

looking for disciples and money.
Many times I confess my own quick
sarcastic stupidity lacks all
sense of tenderness. Many times I
confess I'm scared, a madly lost cat,
a paradox, I'm sorry, really.
But if I close my eyes the horses
are beautiful again; the haunted
hopelessness I can do without. I
must confess I only wish to be
real, authentic, surprising, human
and kind with you in both joy and pain.

The Moon Rose up on Its Tinfoil Bed

and floated along with
us like it was attached
with a string. I thought that
meant we had a boat in
case of emergencies
but she said it was sad

to see it following
in our wake like a cork.
I still think it looked every
bit the stylish silver-
capped swimmer doing
the backhanded tango.

There was no noticeable
splash, ever, but it
did come apart in several
glowing pieces
whenever it hit the
tallest trees, only to

pull itself back into
an almost perfect circle,
albeit a mostly
wobbly one, instantly,
upon clearing
the branches. By midnight

we were the ones dangling
beneath magnetized toes
and being borne along
like a couple of hair
pins. I had to laugh. Your
scarf it was covered in dust.

We Wore Our Hair Long

You don't have to push so
hard. We wore our hair long.
We wanted the animals to trust
us in the wild open spaces.
Everything will come. We wore our
hair long because we wanted to

be able to find our way
back in the moonlight. It'll be
alright. We wore our hair long
because we walked among your

horses and they seemed to think
it was the right thing to
do. You can't take these cosmic
things too lightly. We wore our
hair long because there was no
future left. And because the bullshit

was beginning to pile up

and over our heads like an
avalanche of grey clouds. They offered
us nothing in return for

our broken hearts. This is the
world, they said. We wore our
hair long in spite of robot
armies with falling bombs tattooed on
their metal encased brains. You don't
have to push. We wore our

hair long because we were
in love. It's as simple as
that. We were able to see
all creatures breathing in every

blade of grass. We Wore our
hair long to magnify their tears.
You don't have to push us
so hard. We wanted the animals
to not be afraid to let
us reach them. We wore our hair

long to show the ancient
dragons that we still respected them.
Put your arms around me now.
We were in love. We

wore our hair long as long
as we were together. After that
the poems came like rain. After

that we hit the ground. Please
don't let me hit the ground.
Our hair lit up the sky.

A Dream History of Outer Space

Look. There's just you and me left. All the rest of them
have already given up a long, long time ago. They
dropped their precious, colorful dreams like rusty
railroad lanterns, like abandoned pumpkins, and littered
the

Twitching fields with their tired laughing leaving
footprints. The once-floating music was now broken and
bleeding, jagged like an egg, but the two of us carried
that faithful tune forward in case there were any

Kids like us who still had a beautiful blue spark between
their thumb and forefinger for the earth's future
generation. All the empty seats began to blow away like
paper bags, but the two of us were still holding

Hands with their happy glowing fading ghosts just in
case. The price was a broken heart. One for you. One for
me. That was just the saddest beginning of change. The
awful hairy monsters wrecking

Everything outside the garden gate had heard the hopeful
noise, too, and were hungry for stolen love. They
followed all the faintest footprints back into their sleepy
little homes, into the lost bedrooms, and

Became fixtures in the deep receding shadows there. The
only thing that would save anyone now was a song of
their own. You and I would sit outside their fragile
windows at night and bounce new ideas

Between the ringing stars, hoping to create at least a true
moment of wonder that would wake up any dreamer into
the dream. It's what we do. We were never interested in
capturing any of you. The

Shadows are the ones full of nets. We have no weapons.
We have only ourselves. We say hello again and again.
We say wake up, even inside a boring feeling. We say
write a poem about nothing. We say take a

Long slow walk with a bunch of elephant trees and see
where all the rainbow flowers are going to when they
follow the setting sun. See, you thought this was going to
end in tears, but it's so much more than

That to me, to us, us and them. Because I'm here and still
in love with someone. Because it's my own fingers typing
out your name in front of the whole wide universe in the
morning light like in the movies.

The Gate Before

You were always going
to connect the dots.
I was always going
to overfill a bucket

with poems. You would
eventually drive off waving
your hand like a
star on a spring. I'd

shoulder up another notebook
for the walk. My
hand would rather hold
a pencil. Yours would

accept a kiss from
a perfect stranger. You
were invited to walk
in gardens. I was

given the gate before
we even arrived. You
somehow managed to change
into a diamond, but

in a golden glued-down
seat. I was more
or less a ruby
in a skull's eye-socket

and yet we found
a way to laugh.
That's all I know
of this thing. Now

you sit somewhere outside
the wild feelings blowing
around in my heart,
the photograph of an

ocean entering a dark
green tunnel of a
new amazing day. There's
nothing more to say

that wouldn't take away
its real voice and
replace it with something
less worth listening to.

Fall

Here the three o'clock sun is an old patched-up
fellow with a yellow beard standing in a small
crispy rain of brown leaves, looking
at something that requires a bit
of squinting no one else can
see on the far side of the softening horizon.
You're on your own, he seems to be saying.
He's not even holding a scribbled-upon
piece of broken-off

cardboard, but I can imagine the sad loopy words any
way. I just want you to touch me
with something more comforting than your
spare, unloved money.
I just want to know, someone to tell me,
what ever happened to my own
adventurous heart? Have
you seen it? We were going to see the
whole pageant of the ongoing world of field and

streams. We were going to be young, great praying
dreamers forever. When did we stop
singing together? Here
the sun is lucky to have a pair of
scissor-open shoes to freeze in. He's not wearing a local
sports hat, like the other winds. You're on your own, he
seems to be boasting again. His
lean and faithful dog is waiting to hear his

master's voice saying, come on, come
on let's go. Here the sun is already stiffening
into shade and shadow. Awakening skeletons
are beginning to climb out of
every tree, dropping their bones to the ground
in the sudden snap of the creaking
process like slamming
car doors. The yellow beard points
nowhere in particular,
but nonetheless begs for something less
merciless in the

world before dissolving
into a premature dark silence of
its own whimpering. Here the sun is only half awake as I
turn my head.
No one's there.

Planet Earth

Why must you always jump in with your conclusion?
You're so ready to define the situation that you forget to
remember who we are together—that's always a new
being, one that becomes us only as we connect. I didn't
take that any further because it doesn't warrant it. Either
that being is the absolute better of the two of us or not.
One way we make love, one way we make war. One way
we go to the one-way moon, one way we invade Mars.
One way we duck under the covers, one way we tear up
the garden with our brutalizing machines until every
flower lies dead upon the ground. One way is beautiful,
one is not very pretty, no matter how you look at it. But if
you're in outer space you alone know these things
because they are written in the stars. And here I am
trying to get you to understand something new,
something else
about the way we learn how to feel, even falling through
a barren landscape of violence, a broken heart, even
pushing through a thick, sticky forest of intertwined
fingers at sickening prayer. The real prayer is in how you

live to love, not in how you love to live. I only brought
you here because you mean that much to me. It's our
world. It does not belong to anyone else. They've hijacked
it, yes, but it always disappears right before their very
eyes. Look for the pattern. The pattern is the message.
The pattern is a key. I'm not just doing this for my health.
My number already came up. That leaves you. You know
the drill. There's music to be made. There's magic to be
spoken. There are balances to be restored. You can enjoy
the process you know. You are allowed to experience joy,
but sorrow will have her fair share.

Animal Hospital

We care about you. We care
if you live or die. We
want you to be happy. But
that's not all. We would like
you to sing along. We'd like
you to jump through the hole

in the fence with us. We're
going to free the moon tonight.
We are never coming back here
again, except to rescue any poor
souls who got left behind. It's
a done deal. We are going

to tell the best jokes in
the world just to hear you
belly laugh. We are the healing
that needs to take place. We
are the mysterious force. It's always
been us. We want you to

continue to be you for as
long as you can be. We
carry our internal poets with us
at all times. We are tough
enough for eternity. We are freedom
fighters. And we love to dance.

Elephant with a little Poet on top of its Head

"Every word was once an animal."—Emerson

This circle has been
Broken. The mother has
Disappeared inside the wounds
Of gunfire like an
Eye drop. Who knows if
Any of them limped, crunched,
Down, whole again into the graveyard's
Sacred cusp after that forced

Crawl? If teeth were
Yanked out while they
Were still crying for
Mercy from the poachers?
What makes for a bit
Of elephant luck in the
World today? A mud bath
Or a hard swing of

Trunk into the face
Of a dental hunter?
They are related to
Us through stardust and
Just plain dust. Their children's
Eyes want the same answers
Our own ask. Are we
Loved and can we love?

Or is that too
Much? A passionate life
Filled with passionate kisses,
And hugs from friends?
Without her they must learn
To reinvent the world once
More. There is no time.
The circle's wobbly at best.

It will take years
To find the wisdom
To understand their heart's
Secret language again. She
Used to sing it to them.
It sounded so right. Now
Something's breaking down for both
Of us, Dear Ones.

(Show me the way
you Angels of words
please I pray to
speak and be heard.)

Bone

We built our secret road
and rolled it into a
crumpled ball and pushed it
deep into an empty wine
bottle and dropped it into
the laughing ocean for much,
much later, but like all
young dreams it was found
out by busy strangers and
turned into mounds of vanishing
cash. We still had a
perfect picture of what the
innocent sun looked like through
red broken glass. There's always
something you can do with
the sea and a little
leftover sunlight if you're willing.
Maybe those few drops of
pure dreams were only alive
for those people we were.
I honestly thought we would

help to remember who we
were before the world came
knocking on the door and
took us away in separate
cars. If you cared as
much you would have shouted
something amazing and sweet from
your window. If you cared
you would have thrown something
at me that only I
would ever know how to
catch. I don't blame
them. They are nothing more
than partly animals, nothing more
than hungry, hungry mouths, nothing
more than nibbling plants with
perfumed hidden agendas, but you,
you were a close friend
and that makes things infinitely
worse. The stars grinned all
of a sudden and their
rotten teeth were terrible to
behold and smell. All because
you thought it was all
a sleepy little game to
be dressed up for and
later abandoned to some gruesome
sort of creepy scrapbook for
adults only. I never thought
we'd sink so suddenly into
the solid ground like that.

It didn't make any great
sense to me. Until I
saw your reflection in the
reflection. Then I knew. My
heart snapped in two sad
halves like a broken fish.

The Killers Are Eating

The killers are eating their chili out of bowls
made of bone. Everything in their careless hands is a
hidden weapon. Everything in their smiles is a
sudden weapon. Everything in their sweaty
dreams. Everything in
their wretched lives. Love is a
weapon in their hands. Nothing is seen for what
it is, only for what it can give to
the juicer. The killers are sleeping with their guns
wrapped around themselves. They grind their missing
teeth hard
instead of brushing because only rotten
pain matters. The
sad, reckless killers all live together in a nasty
mess of piss and rice, a nest made of
four sticky walls and some long
forgotten ceilings. They
talk only within shadows to each other. They walk
clumsily forward with writhing shadows hung
around their own
necks like strangling snakes. They are

so much afraid.
They want to die. The killers
are now flushing
their toilets with sandpaper eyes. The
sick killers are starting their cars with nowhere to go but
down. So afraid. So very afraid. With
each passing moment closer and closer to the truth.

Listen To Our Birds

We know a poem isn't going to stop you
from invading our town. It won't get you to
listen to our birds any more than to our
sunsets. That's not why we do it. We know

another poem isn't going to break the blade of
your knife like an invisible karate move. It's not
meant to. What it does is sing, nothing more,
nothing less. It lets loose a certain rhythm, a

back beat, that's all. It provides a place for
a single voice to exist among the annihilation and
carnage of endless war. It carries the words of love
to always new ears. It doesn't strap on bombs

before it goes to marketplace. You don't find it,
it finds you. We know a poem won't stop
you from rigging the election, from buying the favors of
bad men, from selling out
people for profit.

All it does is sing, and sing, and sing
some more. If this irritates you, we're so sorry
for the rather rude inconvenience of our humming
together for peace. We know a poem is not going

to stare down a tank barrel for too long.
We get it. Sooner or later you're going to
have to look at your million-dollar watch and
make a million-dollar nasty decision before it gets

too late for any decent dinner-time. There are those who
are with you all the way to the
proverbial bank. They'd like to use all those annoying
poems for some kind of ballistic target practice.

We know a poem isn't your thing. You can't tell
us apart. You think we all look the same.
Of course this is all part of the ongoing
sadness created when you ignore
the poem's sound.

We know a poem isn't going to make us
any new friends. We've all known a poem that
was burned in your bonfires. But did you know
this one is for you? It's about feeling something.

The Matter

I would want you to be as happy at the
end as at the beginning. I would want the courage
that you found to be as natural as your high
when you can't help yourself.
I would want the thrills
to be all your moment like a panoramic view from
the lighthouse of the heart. I would want to feel
the happiness in your fingertips
as we walked along the
edges of your own shoreline. I would want you to
feel at home in your own gait, your own laughter,
your own stance. The poem
wouldn't adorn you as much

as fly by you and give you its wind, wave
you its wing on a nodding shaft of sunlight. I
wouldn't want you to be
named after any star because
that field could not begin
to account for the amazing

blue depth in your eyes to me. I would want
you to be able to dance with every adventurous drop of
rain. I would want you to be free to
explore your own strength for
beauty. I would want you
to climb into my arms for naked peace, with fun
goodwill, but not without a
healthy curiosity. I would want

you to always be the person inhabiting your soul. I
would want you to be
still growing into yourself even
at your age. I would want you to disregard these
crazy ramblings and kiss me over and over again. I
would want you to be anything you want to be
and not what any poet wants you to be. I
would want you to be
surrounded by caring friends who
could never harm you. I would want you to be
your own poet, although I'm
more than happy to step
into the role when you need me, but you don't.

Consider this a letter of
resignation. I'm honored by your
presence. It's the surest proof
that love is worth every
humiliation, every trip and fall,
every injury and setback. I
would only want you to be careless as well as
careful when it comes to matters of the heart. You

will know what I mean when you are standing at
the crossroads. Trust in yourself
first. Safety is as much
an illusion as anything else with bars on the door.
I would want you to be the one who gets
the job of living well
done with kindness and mercy.

I would want you to be engaged with the energy
that heals the world. I would want you to be
the last human being standing.
I've said about all there
is to say. I just wanted you to know. These
words are all I have to hold you with now.
I want you to be blessed one more time. It's
important to me. Otherwise I
wouldn't say it. I would
want you to be smiling as you read this. It
is real if we make it an action toward being
so. I would want you to be sure and ready.

Big Escape

Oh nothing's wrong. Everything
walks its own immanent brand
of magic through each new day's
front doors. But that doesn't mean

a heart isn't sliced down the
middle by some remembered
sunset. We're all clothes inside
the washing machine. And still

you see people acting like
sharks, just like animals with
poisonous barbs for fingers
looking for something to spear

just for the hell of it. They
take the most beautiful thing
they can find and break it. So,
no, nothing's wrong. Amidst all

this idiot carnage I
have you pretending to have
all the time in the world to
find and give love. You think that

those stars don't ever lie, but
of course they are becoming
the bells that will toll your sleep.
There you go again turning

me out, living a life while
I'm breaking down in my strides
becoming nothing more than
a vanishing cloud of dreams.

No One Will Ever Give You This Poem

and say did you know it was written for
you? But I will. No one will walk up to
you on the street one day and say he loved
you so. But I'm telling you now. What good

would a pyramid be or a hanging
garden or a starry night without your
delightful creases capturing the songs
in their own wondrous folds? I want to be
where you are. Not to travel not to stand

before a charming place nor to be present
where you are not but always where you are.
What good would it do flying in a car
or on the back of a horse or sleeping
under an arousal of spread leaves if

there was not your arm to touch your hair to
sift next to mine your face to press against?
I get it now. That song. Nothing Compares.

How'd I come to this edge of particular notions?
A little bit more and I'll be buzzing

to pieces a lost moment then I'll be
becoming from a completely different
angle and you'll be living still in
the same world as my love. Somebody please
find her and give her her poem. Do this

for me. She is the only reason I
believe in this world. Anyone can view
this story. I was once with her without
her. There was no other way. I know she
deserves real truth. Crack open this heart then

eat what's left together. But that's for later.
Right now I just want you to know that
these feelings exist in our time. May I
never utter a false dream again but
always keep that name where I am going.

Mirror

Take these pretty poetry things before
they are finished, you know you
want to. Take all the pale
fingers fluted with rings, the nails
becoming visible at last like the
sails of great ships, the bones

beneath the waves holding the life-force
in its place, ripe with pulsating
branches of many bells, and eat
them, drink them, become them. Take
as many tall trees as you
can and stuff them into the

cotton bags of clouds like dried
snakes. Take clouds and float them
across a mirror. Take a river
then and pour it on your
hair like a silk scarf and
laugh out loud. Throw your head

back, open up your throat like
never before and finally lighten up
the night like a good little
star. Of course they won't listen.
But put your hands deep into
the fields of stars and pull out

all the moons you are meant
to know, and get to know
them. Remember this, a garland of
all the roses in all the world isn't enough.
The streaming morning
sun isn't enough. Only love's enough.

Folded Up

Time to pull in the shining teeth,
but it makes me so sad, you know
I'd rather be holding hands. The
others have told me, don't hold back,
hit them with every white knuckle,
and let them bleed out, I'd rather
be kissing your face. It hurts, you're
killing me, and all I want to
do is have that dance under the
perfect wolf-licking moon. And now
I suppose every corner must
be folded up, secretly put
away somewhere. They told us, they
told me, nothing lasts. After that
you go back to darker dreaming,
if you are lucky. If not, well,
you know in your bones which bells are
still ringing and which have lost their
silvery will to make something
beautiful crawl out of nothing

more than the air and the ghosts of
certain leaves. Now I'm on the path
of too many broken things, and
walking with my twisted feet, my
revolving head, looking for the
red town where you used to live in
a silent window with curtains.

Our Love Is Enough

To stop the world from exploding
Like Krypton. It has to be.
Like purple flowers we're there on
Burnt battlefields. It raises its flag,

Too, and continues the march toward
The dreaming sun in spite of
All the smoke and ash this
World has to offer. Our love

Is enough to weather the ice-
Cold precipitation of all loud hateful
Partiers above and below the radar
Of kind thinking. It has to

Be. Our love is enough to
Set free the zoo animals. Our
Love is enough to protect the
Creature that contains all sea creatures

From irreparable harm. It has to
Be. Our love is enough to
Filter the smog into breathable air
Again. Our love is enough to

Write the poems that witness the
Whole truth and not just some
Of the lies that are bought
And sold on the nightly news

Like used cars. It must be.
Our love is enough to turn
Back the four horsemen and their
Spaceships, turn them back into constellations,

Back into fireflies. Our love is
Enough to ensure that walls and
Bridges are there to welcome strangers
And not to incite greedy tendencies.

It has to be. Our love
Is there to remind us to
Always be creative givers. Our love
Is enough. Our love is enough.

Weeds of the World, Unite!

We invade the invaders and
they invade us, these little
blooming weeds. They raise five
flowers and let them blow
into the winds like fleets
of stars. All of us
steer by their turning tide.
All of us will eventually
fall by their shining example
into wintry skies, crisp and

dispersing everywhere like snow, but
they do not give up
that ghost. Instead they regrow
even the frozen toes of
heaven into an eruption of
abundant walking shoes, the kind
to take you wherever you
are going, and with whom.
this is the miracle of

green life. It exists solely

to exist. It will not
take no for an answer.
It sucks sunshine like it's
going out of style and
spits it back out in
puffs of pure oxygenated cookies,
baked to perfection and ready
to eat. And once inside
of your guts it works
its ancient magical spell like

clockwork, restoring even the most
cynical nature back to its
original joy in simply breathing
again. And then of course
comes another blast on the
field from all the trumpets
at hand to signal the
war is not yet over
For some of us, we
must go on to the

gates of forever, some alone
and some of us together.
At either end the greening
will take its rightful place
in the conversation about the
meaning of all love within
the meaning of all life.

And because of that this
poem finds its way to
you today, making so sure.

Morning Comes

Morning comes pouring itself slowly up the road
Like a familiar figure you recognize even before
You can make out any of its features.
You know the gait. You're acquainted with the

Certain slope of its shoulders. And you begin
To wonder if it will make it all
The way to your doorstep with this carefully
Packaged box of new day or not. But

It's a steady come on, even in the
Misty rain. It's a sure bet even in
The barking wind's manic persistence to stop and
Play, to pet and hug. Morning moves with

Trained purpose like a dancer among stars. Like
A dolphin beside a cruise ship. The comforting
Sound is subtle, but undeniably close, and getting
Closer yet, until you find yourself back to

Life, back to being ready for anything that
Just so happens to look like a movement
In the right direction. And just as quickly
Morning is nothing more than a dot of

Drying color on the canvas of the trees,
Lifting away to join with all the blue
Heads of angels making the clouds waft their
Perfumes around and around
like roasted heavenly beans.

Letter(s)

The sky set itself on fire, but
it really didn't make a difference. Birds
knew not to worry any more than
usual. Trees thought and made the most

of their landscapes as a way of
being modern and yet timeless. It's only
people who suffer from too much starlight
and not enough moon. The oceans continue

to gulp their own feelings like blue
ice. You and I make our musics
and leave the singing to somebody else.
We count off the same steps of

our eventual dissolving like petals given like
wishes to the wind, like hats blown
into another time and space. Again it
was that sky choosing to live in

a mirror rather than putting on shoes
that caused the day to crackle and
explode. We put our heads into our
hands like letters found in the attic.

A List of Some People

Some people got lost. Some
people are still falling
down. People were blown clean
off. Some people fled.

Some people buried their
own evenings in good
excuses. Some people
became a myth. And some

people knew better. Some
people starved some people
with lies; those people
killed us quite easily.

Some turned to look back. Some
waved their blinking flashlights
in our faces like hearts
beaming smoke signals. Some

people can take the pain
away. We need to thank
them. Some people haven't
been here since John. And all
being flawed, people take
flight and walk away to
their own clouds. People are
start-to-finish humble spies.

Poem for the Poet

—for Bill Yarrow

Poetry is a way of breathing
against the enemy's chest without
losing consciousness again. It
is a ghost dance. Poetry is to
be determined by the plight of bees.

Poetry is a waterfall on
a mailing list. I've never tasted
a finer whiskey than poetry.
Poetry is half immersed in mud
and water. Poetry's my dragon.

Poetry leaps to its feet and hails
Death's stealth riders as cowards and fools.
That's pretty cool. It emerges as
that unraveling feeling for the
new century of love. Poetry's no

military salute to speak of,
(thank God for any human mischief!)

takes the guesswork out of looking an
elephant in the eye by seeing
no citizen of the stars as a

mere foreigner. Poetry
has no government behind it dressed
all in black. Poetry's a pierced copper
small animal weather vane among
other presently punch-drunk things.

Wild Geranium (Crane's Bill)

I don't want to be the guy
sneaking like a thief who says
words don't mean we care. I don't
want to be the one cutting
like a throat who says our ghost

is lifting out of this life. Don't
want to be the one who says
all talk's another flight risk.
The one like a cop saying
look away close your eyes that

swan's trumpet is too scared to
sound off. I don't want to be
the one who bets gravity
is a grandfather clock thrown
into the ocean. I don't want

to be the one shrinking like
a vampire who shouts stars are

nothing but holes cut out of
the fabric of our dreams, who
states, I'll never give my heart

a melody of its own
to sway with, says our chance
is a folding campfire chair,
one who like a barfing moon
says this is the last best dance.

Treatise on Some Blue Skies

It's true, what they say, love
is the only thing that
makes any sense. It is
the bravest thing any
of us will do. But it's
impossible, dangerous,
stupid. I don't want
you to trip into its
beautiful trap without

me. Like being swallowed
by a fish, I'm told, yes
actually I know
there is no warning that
would matter any way.
No one is going to
look away. Love wins. It's
just that awful. You will
disappear from view and

later be found wandering
around with a far-
away look in your eyes.
It's incredibly self-
centered in its hunger.
Never want you to have
to use a cane just to
cross the street to get to
the fair. This thing will hit

like a meteorite.
You'll see people walking
with craters where their hearts
used to be. Numb individuals
with painful
looking brows. But please don't
listen to me. It's best
if you choose your own set
of deepest feelings over

me. No warning will translate
past love's hypnotic
thump on the head. And perhaps
it shouldn't. You don't
want to miss out on the
rare chance to fall into
blue skies. I'm sorry. Look,
this poem's just a song
I wrote with your moon.

The Subsequent Ferocious Silence Is

just another torn & burning journey
flag for the rebel heart. All we know for
sure is that dancing among the toads and
crickets takes a bit of courage. Beauty takes

real living guts these days. Laughing takes guts,
too. Living takes love. Love is feeling. What'd
you think I was going to say? This is
not some lame-ass joke about building art

out of tiny silver bells, my friends, or
putting two hands and two hands together.
Takes all your free will, causes centuries
of prickly pain, often doesn't give you

any cause for hope--you are an easy
target just like me I suppose--but I
will, we will. Yet a kiss will do wonders
nonetheless. It does not take hiding for

a living. Seriously hiding should
always be a temporary fix for
the sadness only. Okay? Takes a lot
of imagination. Education

it does not take. Imagination takes
guts. I read books, so what do you do with
them? Reading takes guts. It doesn't take a
steep discount on the price of your next beer.

Living can be lonely. It doesn't
always include enough sleep. It takes hugs,
but sometimes all you get is bugs. It does
not take guns—no matter what they show you

on the news. That's just them thinking about
more and more sex. Sex takes guts. It does not
take a James Bond film. A James Bond film takes
some guts. What? Did you think I wouldn't go

there? Oh ye of little faith. Thinking takes
guts. You have a mind of your own. Aren't you
the lucky one? Living can be lucky
I guess, but it doesn't always include

the right street to meet your audience on.
That's all I'm going to say for now, so
what are you going to do about it?
Doing something takes guts you know. What it

doesn't take is the proper shoes. Sometimes

the proper shoes just don't fit the person
wearing them. And being a person takes guts,
all kinds of guts, versus all kinds of the

darker nightmare bacterium within
and without you. Here are a few of the
truest facts: Sunday in the afternoon,
March, carrying a tune from the same dream.

Flower Power

"Poets are damned but they are not blind, they see with
the eyes of the angels."—William Carlos Williams

There is something beautiful I want to say
to you that doesn't seem to make much
more sense in a box of clever words
like this one. It feels closer to words

than not words, but more like what you
might expect me to grunt or groan up
real close—stuck on or against almost—to
a huge sky full of clearly-ripened opening

stars. I've been there before you see, so
the whole thing is neatly tattooed in my
invisible head at all times, like a benevolent
trauma. It has already become me. What that

means is every now and then I can

look straight down at my writing hands, even
my arms, and see there a pulsating Milky
Way stretched beneath, inside. I don't know if

that is a bad or a good sign,
but it doesn't feel too bad, just strange.
But it does give me some point of
reference for what I'm trying to send off

to you right now. Poets are always trying
to share words that are made from what
it feels like to be next to another,
altogether different feeling than the one they are

supposed to be experiencing. They can't help it—
it's what they do. It's neither clever nor
particularly inventive, but it can be sparkling, and
perhaps that is the meaning of any flower.

This particular one is for you, that I
am sure of, even if I'm not sure
of its hidden fragrance. That it got all
on its own. Like you'd want it to.

I Want To Sing To You

without looking at the words. I want to draw
a picture of you
without setting my hat on fire. I want to swing you
around in an open field
without thinking something's bound to go wrong. I want
to touch your hands
without resorting to an old map found buried in a book
on fairies.

To run with you in the downpour without looking for a
quick-squeezed
way in. Want to remember your face because it's resting
in my fingers like a cherry
pit. I want to sit with you in front of the ocean without
planning
to take one shell. I want to find you in a garden

without thinking I should remove my shoes first and put
them under a rose bush

for safe keeping. I want to give you that dance without
dropping all blanks
in the chamber for good luck. I want to embrace your
name without
falling into an unmade ditch of spears head first. Want to
drink your

trance without going home and putting myself to bed
afterwards. I want to
play my guitar like a wounded warrior without having to
explain the nature of all scars.
I want to leave my most careless poems on your doorstep
without having
to fold up all the moonbeams into neat little rows before
I go.

I Want You

to have something, but I don't think
you need anything from me. There are
poems that belong in your hair and
no one else's. They should be like
stars that only appear every
one thousand years, and even then can
only be seen when you are walking

next to the ocean. You make them
shine. And you don't even have to
try. There's more truth to your presence for
me than a sunrise because the warmth
I feel is in my whole being.
Tell me how do you thank someone
for something like that? I know your life

has its own set of sorrows, but I
also know that you face them with
a dignity that is who you
are. I know you have cried real tears. I
know your heart has ached away the hours

before. These words are only a
small breath to cool your current burns,

but they are given without debt, and
without want. They are words that say they
will always believe in you no
matter what, that's all. Please take them.
Apply them whenever you need to.
They are all I have. You've already
given me the meaning I sought.

War and Peace

War

The once shining lake was
busy draining itself. All the
better cared for boats were
looking like disjointed discarded single
shoes in a messed up paint
chipped closet. No one was
thinking well okay a leaky
sole is better than a
wounded heel. You get the
picture, it was pure roadkill.
Turns out war causes
everyone to turn into their
favorite cartoon animals. That part
they got right. They were
right to draw it on
all the crumbling buildings and
more than right to reward
it with its own special

day with masks and everything,
but you couldn't convince the

public. Nothing convinces the public.
All they want out of
this particular post life is
to bite down into something
warmish and finish the whole
argumentative night off with a
great big slice of Fall
TV shows. Hey, they voted
for it on both sides
of the Atlantic. Only some
of us chose to listen
to some new music, not
the kind you have to
dress up for, but the
kind you have to show
up for inside of yourself,
to wake up to. Well
perhaps that's too sarcastic if
you care what other people think,
it's not meant to be,
it's only a tiny pebble
rolling down an ancient hill
after all. The real mudslide
began a long time ago
when the dinosaurs decided to
evaporate and the hordes of
walking fish decided to investigate
the mountains of trash left

over from that startling
exit to see if they
might have an appetite for
monumental change, too. Then we
came charging along with our
viciously trained tanks rolling over
everything and flattening the script.
If we had found a
way to also roll up
the sky it would have
been done, to hang on
some guy's wall while he
masturbates to Wagner. Again, too
cruel or too polite? The
war brought us together. It
forced us into a hole.
It washed us out again
and again. We gathered our
things and told our feet
to not look back, but
some did any way. We
believed the strangest things, too.

Peace

They brought their own sorcerer to
the table to try to
cheat the truth out of seeing
its own reflection, but the
good guys were always relaxed enough
to know when to

get the shotguns down from above
the fireplace. They can smell
the deceit like it is burning
right under their noses, even
if it's planned in an office
on Wall Street months

in advance. They make the necessary
sounds of joy and offer
that incense to the Great Spirit
rather than wait to be
ambushed by unscrupulous con men who
like to collect power

jolts like vintage automobiles. All of
your stuff will be divided
and sold when you are dead,
it will lose its resemblance
to you and become nothing more
than petrified veins to

be mined by workers who would
rather kill sacred trees than
starve. They're not the problem. Snakes
are not the problem. Sharks
are not the problem. Guns are
not the problem. You

have to be able to walk
right up to them and
smile and mean it, even when
they turn into hideous monsters
without any pity in their pale
watery eyes. You have

to know the truth, even when
they offer you everything for
nothing. You have to see the
beautiful horizon inside them, the
same sun, the impossible light, then
you may have a

chance to actually sit down and
talk. You might even make
bees move out of the way

so you can taste the
honey without getting stung, and more
importantly without harming the

bees. Then everybody goes back to
their business with renewed interest.
Because nothing was chosen over someone
else's home. Nothing was invaded.
Nothing was destroyed. The only thing
that was done was

a story was told that included
everybody in their own skins.
It proves it can be done.
But not if you come
to the table already armed with
hatred. You will be

caught in the nose hairs of
the chief and disqualified of
your power like a child. Yet
like a child you may
begin again in wonder and be
glad. Hear it again.

Hello

Hello is the one thing
that isn't loaded with stuck-up
false notions. Hello isn't yet
capable of sweetly lying to your
eyes. It hasn't the nerve.

Hello, let's open the possibility
that some things are worth
believing without a shred of
asking for the inevitable ruined return
to spoil the moment. Hello

acknowledges the metaphysics of immediate
joy. It accepts the
understanding. Like a deep breath
hello breaks into the room by
walking through its walls. Hello

doesn't hate goodbye. It carries the will to
connect all

sinews by the cord of
years found inside every shared moment.
Hello pulsates. Hello's magic lives

to perform, but it's not
a trick, it's a natural
progression towards painting the picture.
Hello is all I've got. You're the
one with more to offer.

That Rare Moment

Words are only the windows
I want you to look through
right now. Mostly because they
can give you a sensing key
to unlock the many rooms
of my feelings. Don't worry. It's
nothing more than a vase
for some flowers, a glass for
some spilled sunlight. I know
it's momentary for you. But you
can't pretend in the face
of the big reveal, or else
everything falls apart, and that
would make a disastrous picture of
a singular spectacular sky. I
don't know where the brightness comes
from that illuminates you to
me. I mean I know it
is you, but it is
also me, some part of me
that recognizes in your voice,
in your face, in your hair

a movement that gives me
a raw courage I never knew.
So the words become like
curtains, they are meaningless in themselves.
They need these alphabetical walls,
the whole spinning language outside streaming
through the inner airways to
make their introductions, to ask you
to dance. That's its whole,
strange phenomenon, like a favorite song,
you just can't help but feel
fantastic in its presence if only
for that rare moment it
plays around in your head. The
silly artistic purpose here is only to not be a liar.
The real purpose here is
to be authentic as we live
and breathe. The personal purpose
is to be honest without faking
a special boredom with you.
I didn't make this up. The

world existed well before the
spark created by our crossing paths.
I felt it enough to
bleed forth this poem. You may
not have noticed it happening
at all. That's not my problem,
But it is my mortal
awareness, owned or disowned, soul-wise
speaking for the taking. It

shouldn't matter to you. I'm only
saying you made a big
difference in my heart that deserves
a little notice of thanks
on my part. You probably receive
these kinds of awards daily.
I'm more than happy to add
mine to the shelf because
it certainly belongs there among all
the others, but I will
not be lumped in with the
strangled stars when I am
the one bringing you the moon.

I Don't Know What to Say

But it all works out. Truth is something I'm sure
I've never seen, but the more time goes on, the
Less I'm inclined to believe in it. Still I don't want
To be one of those giving the finger to God
And begging for a showdown
With an army of unfeeling

Angels. We were kicked out of heaven for having a
Healthy curiosity about the taste
Of things as they weren't ever really
Presented to us. I think we made the right choice.
Taste buds demanded their freedom,
And from there it was
Only a matter of time
Before others followed their prime

Example. Eyes, ears, lips, fingers,
Hair follicles all wanting to
Know more, more about the
Winds, more about the sun

And the rain, more about
Themselves among the stars. It's
Okay to feel things more
Deeply than ever before. We
Choose to break the rules. It wasn't by accident. We

Wanted to know the rough
Unexpected skin of the road
We were on, even if it went unraveling under the
Doorway like a broken dam. We wanted to lift our
Unadorned faces up into the
Sky without flinching from fear.
That's the key. We don't
Want to live with nightmares of

Being thrown into a ditch for being out of line.
I created my own lines here. They may not make
A lot of sense to you right now, but I
Think you'll enjoy the flowers in the end. If not
There are plenty of other
Gardeners, including you, who are

Willing to grow something else
For everyone. Either it's free
Or it's not. And that has nothing to do with
The cost. It's just an attitude, even as you are
Buying or selling the goods. I don't know what to
Tell you that you haven't already thought of all by

Yourselves. We are fallen from
Grace, but we are always

Happily weaving our poems any
Way. We are still holding
Onto sweet faces like jugs
Of lifesaving water and drinking
Deeply the impossible beautiful light
From each other's eyes. That's
Enough to prove to me this life is long enough.

Crumpled

We wanted so much to find ourselves
in a beautiful world. It was, and
is, but every inviting leaf has
got another hidden dangerous
precedent that must be surrendered
to in order to survive to see
another sunset with the ones you
actually love. It's always been

nothing more than a tired struggle just
to snuggle and mean it when words fail
to give glad meaning to what's truly
happening. Maybe in school you can
look around and see many different
levels of life changing, it's mind, but
somewhere in the real world it's mostly
car after car driving into tall

mirrors at sadder and sadder speeds.
You don't want to hear this and I don't
want to say this, the alternative

is to become their puppets, perform
their silly dances on the blood soaked
streets like pieces of crumpled paper.
We are not just monkeys looking for
the toss of a coin into our cups.

Vanishing Vapors with Van Gogh

These clouds are what I have
with me. Their language is mine
but it is drying today as
we speak. I catch the darkening
sparks, but that's not to be
your concern. I am sure you
shall go on. What I want
is to deliver your song. I
doubt it is for anybody else.
Clouds are good at pretending. Don't
they know why I'm making all
these cryptic statements? I suppose they
add up to something being said.
Clouds make me want to hide
but not because I'm sad. These
ones have chosen me without knowing
me, yet my choice is out in
the open. This mass has no

place in my loneliness, but here
they swarm like huge golden flies.
The clouds give no sign of
love--is that too much of
an ache I wonder? I hope
they know they are appreciated.

Clouds are all I have to keep
my need at bay, and I am
feeling like this poem any way.
Sitting and staring at their ambiguity
I find I'm still where I
am, waiting for the actual, honest

shake from someone. The spots have
changed. There are no longer steps
to climb, only disembodied lost houses.
Clouds have joined with something far
off now, flying away. For clouds
have done their best, it is.

The Poor Dumb Creature

was dead, with a spear stabbed in its fat head
and hung from a pole like an upside down
clay flag. The dumb creature who had killed the
beautiful one was grinning from ear to
ear like a flickering cat. And as I

studied the body I thought about the
natural grace it must have taken to
move it through all that water for all those
many years, stay alive, to actually
grow that large. Now it was no more than

a black and white trophy for a picture,
its softening head making a crushing
dent on a wooden rug, it's flopped fin a
useless arm pulled through a rope, and nothing
more. On TV police cars were burning

like grotesque candles in a macabre
storefront window, on main
street smashed open stores

were being looted and tear gas bombs were
being sprayed like confetti on fed-up
balling, sad protesters. Two hate crimes were

committed. Only one was ever known,
truly decided. Another young man
is dead on our streets. It took seven mad,
brutal bullets to wake up a partly
slumbering country to its own petty

indifference. Those who protect us did
not protect us. Those who serve us did not
serve these. Our lost children are not being
respected. Any harm done harms us all.
Politicians are quick to pass out some

newly minted campaign slogans instead
of genuine outrage or concern. But
the people became the living symbols
of a nation that has a voice. Lets hope
that walk is heard deeply in our bravest new heart.

Birds Fly

Birds fly and people focus on finding their still
point. Birds fly and
people wait for love, but I couldn't.
Birds fly and people think about beauty. Birds
fly and people become frustrated.
Birds fly and people drown in little rooms. Birds fly and
people
like strange words cast huge shadows. Birds fly and
people
make mocking landscapes filled with balloons. Birds fly
and

people frighten themselves in the mirror. Birds fly
and people fold like origami horses. Birds
fly and people ask for blessings under their breath.
Birds fly and people die of old age on fire escapes.
Birds fly and people will take horrible vacations
in their mind's lonesome valleys. Birds fly and people are
programmed to be the problem.
Birds fly and

people don't remember soon enough. Birds fly and
people pour a glass of water. Birds fly and people
hurry in the wind and rain like it's a matter
of pity. Birds fly and people run on the
grass until there's nothing left but bones. Birds fly and
people go down the stairs. Birds fly and people say little
to each other. Birds fly and people wave.

Like a Pop Song This is the Head of a Sunflower

This is the head of a sunflower as well
as the butt of a beetle as well as
the membrane with its busy veins
of traffic between
sky and cloud as well as
the upside-down skeleton
of a raindrop as well as the groove twisting

in a line around your sweet
kissable thumb as
well as the balding white spot
scuffed atop the
toe of your mowed-down old
moose slippers as
well as the polished slick talons on the eagle
somewhere pumped up from the kill
as well as

the moment the feeling flag slaps
its stitches against

the pant legs of the day
begging for an ice cream
as well as a tired old poet making a
sad grunting noise through his chin
as he types
with one finger as well as
the colorless mass

of cocoons blowing away on any
given spring day
and turning into flowers tying on
their new bonnets
as well as you still crammed into my heart
like a folded map I've kept for all these
years or a message I've never been able to

code out or like some pyramid
on the horizon
I just can't seem to ignore
anymore even though
I want to as well as the milky way flying
through outer space like a swirling rush
of water all
lit up from within from its
own blushing crush

on life as well as this unwieldy ball of
sentences as well as this fishing line cast into
the unknowable electric currents of now
and never and
maybe forever eh as well as a tiny spastic

hope clinging to a fast falling building as well

as any dream lingering on the edge of sanity
as well as the boy who forgot to go
home and grow up as well as the girl
who fingered her hair and smiled at the boy
as well as vanished years that
tumbled into rainbows

Actual Reality

Travel into the beautiful swirling being
you occupy whenever you get the
chance. It's your right to seek
the name of the most holy
one in your deepest awakening. Then

will you most likely find fellow
travelers splashing about in their naked
auras in the Milky Way's fist
full of molecules like any other
happy otters made of moon beams

and eternal star dust. To look
directly at the universe is not
an original sin, but it is
or it isn't a formidable, dangerous
path to cross blue and red

trains with at the next natural
wiring station . Just because it's blessed
doesn't mean it can't be compromised

or binding. Greed can bring a
redwood to its knees. All you've

got to do is accept the
risk with an open heart and
quit mumbling, use an open mind
before you go in all the
way and remember to always love

where you are every living thing
you encounter for its own shining
soul. And where souls touch is
the trembling truth being born again.
Each form brings delight to the

Sun. But the darkness would rather
crush you. You, however, cannot be
crushed forever because nothing is extinguished;
only hidden. It's okay to laugh.
It's okay to dance. It's okay

to sing, to make music that
others might consider noise. It's okay
to not make sense. Okay to
drum your fingers on the rocks.
To dream. To imagine. To be

a poem. To turn into a
bird or a cloud. To wear
a cloak of many stars. To
return to yourself at last. Der
dust, dust, dust, dust, dust, dust.

A Prisoner Refuses to Eat

They have placed a
gun on every table.
I don't want to
kill you for supper.

They have thrown a
net around every tree.
I don't want a
sky made to order.

They have stolen a
child from every heart.
I do not believe
in this long mirror.

They've become us when
it suits their purpose.
I do not want
to answer that calling.

What I want is

not anything that's made
but looks a lot
like your smiling eyes.

It is in fact
most like a laughing
voice or the yellow
sun blown across daisies.

If It's Not Love Maybe

it's your iPad. If it's
not love it's your iPhone.
If it's not love what have
we got? If it's not love
it's the philosophical

elephant in the
automated sea. If
it's not love what was the
question? If it's not love
what was your laughter for?
If it's not love it's the

last lemon. If it's not
love it's all strangers in
the grass. If it's not love
it's living alone in
the city. If it's not
love it's not your destiny.

If not love not for

the real you. If it's not
love can the universe
be trusted with caring
for us? I've no answer.
If it's not love I quit.

Apis Indica

I really don't
have the heart to
try and write the
love you deserve
anymore. It's
taken everything,
every breath, every
circle around

the sun, just to
hold the pen against
the paper.
I know you want
it all and I'm
much less than whole.
I'm like a moon
stuck in one year,

illumined, but
stopped and chipping.

You've still got plenty
of stars to
be swimming through.
All I can bring
you now is a
slight dusting of

the same light you've
already seen
blowing across
these waves. Go now.
Swim that damned channel
before we're sunk
too deep to rise
again in Spring.

The Sky Here's Full Stopped

under a blanket of
blue snow. That's my
reality. But even if
one of those thread-like

clouds throws its swallowed
light after you I
suppose I'd be happy.
I want your footsteps
illumined on the path.

And if one wild
wind might detach itself
from today's army to
gently brush back the
hair from your cheeks,

well, you know, I
think maybe what's left
of all the free
floating leaves in the
world could not possibly mind.

Fog

I miss you in the pizza box
and in the paper plates.
I miss you in the silverware
that sits alone and waits.

I miss you in that flour moon
so spilled upon the gates.
I miss you in the stars tonight
that spell out hopes and fates.

I miss you in the mirror round.
I miss our sheets unfurled.
I miss you in that Beatle sound
that used to save the world.

It is who I am, what I do.
I miss you as before
like rain that splatters through the peephole
and scatters to the floor.

Sometimes I forget

how strange the world is. I'm not so worried
about following your rules. I'm much
more interested in
being real. I've never believed in
their definitions of
beauty. Yet already I've seen many
miraculous things on
just about every surface. I figure it's some kind
of minute mojo being more like
cosmic patterns upon
another wall somewhere. It's all made
out of the
same stuff. But even that's not the whole truth.
In order to get there we'd have to go
everywhere at once. And yet we dance! I don't
have to give you this poem any more than
you have to read it. The sun will burn
out when the sun will burn out. Until then
you have to continue to climb out of yourself
into the open air so to speak. The story
simply unfolds around you a million

times a second
like a pretty difficult puzzle but is it fun
or can it be? And still we kill each
other. That's the really sad part. We don't even

know any other way. Oh sure there are many
here among us who refuse to fight but they
end up dying any way. There's a point to
all these words but you're crazy if you think
it's up to me to tell

you what that
means. I'm not that voice but I hear it
too. It's coming out of every rock, every drop
of rain,every flower, every particle of air, every
stitch of clothing, every cell of skin, every bead
upon our silly heads. We take it all way
too seriously. Nothing's ever going to stop the gate
from closing in on us but we could have
a picnic among the rising stones and later count
as many stars as there are souls of beings.

Sweeteners

They drop themselves right
into the mix like
parachuting seeds, only
these pods they

spring from are the
everyday open
doors we all pass through on
our way to and

from breaths. Ah, why call it
anything else
but ordinary, this miracle
life?

The Last Time

we met you wanted to
be hungrily kissed in
the dark with a small moon
for your only pillow
and just stars for your billowing
nightgown. How am I
to go forward with so
much sweet chaos in my
mind? I am wrecked upon
your lips like a delirious
dilapidated
old sailor who embraces
the surrounding
sea like it's an arrow
through a sad and thirsty heart.

Long Distance

Here's the thing. I never thought you'd
Be swept away from me for always at a time. Some
Grain of you always seems to catch
In my eyes from time to time.
What I'm trying to say is I'm
Sorry that we are no bigger than our
flesh. I'd give anything to be in
Your presence without history or seasons having
Been hammered like nails into our hearts. I understand
That oceans will continue to live and
Die in our veins, but also clouds
Will rise out of our many done deeds to
Drench us sooner or later. I want
You to let go of me completely
Now, and know that you are forever loved.

"No honest poet can ever feel quite sure of the permanent
value of what he has written: he may have wasted his time and
messed up his life for nothing."—T.S. Eliot

The Horse-Shaped Hole

stands softly in moon-wash
nibbling on tufts at
the top of sleeping
day. Instantly we are
deputized astronomers bearing silent
witness. No one knows
what true colors the
animal exhibits. None care.

Shaking his great shaggy
mane back and forth
he releases an army
of tiny bright things

that begins floating toward
that orb like a
thousand naked canoes. He
lifts a hoof, the

sky flushes itself and
sequinned as any old

dancer begins to fold
upon deeper and deeper

swirls. Wings flutter within
all the invisible trees
for miles around. Nothing
winks out. Instead

everything's neatly lit by
the mere fact of
this moment like a
candle in the clouds.

In Memory of Lily Burk

I don't know what they want. Anything you
give them will never do. Most fear pain
because they cause it. Hate happens over and

over. As if they have two nostrils but
no real experience of air. This is beyond
sad belief. The apple hits the ground no

matter how many times you drop it. They've
failed to connect this in their brains and
so are heartless like zombies who want but

cannot produce life. Instead they attack a young
girl on an errand for her mother and
force her to die like a butterfly pinned

to the dirty wheel of sensation. And for
what? To get close to the moon? To
lay their heads upon the liar's tongue? Apples

tremble on tiny stems. Oh Love get here
first. Oh Love get here first. Oh Love
get here first. Oh Love get here first.

They Don't Get to Say Everything

The world hasn't ended. Your part in it is still ongoing.
The going on world hasn't winked out. Every possibility
is still out there. In there out there it doesn't matter
where you are. The here
and now claims you only for the tribe. They only want
someone to tell them they are wrong.
Well. They are very wrong. They want war to come and
kill them. It's a suicide in a gummy side
show tent. Love can't be coerced. Like gravity
it works every time that conditions are present. Right left
it doesn't matter where you stand
when peace is blooming. The center holds you
tight to itself like a granulated belt strap. You can use it to
get stronger than you are. You can
use it to navigate a star made of
rooms. You can use it to climb up whole mountains. You
can use it to fill in a
hole of your own making. You can be digested or
expelled from its hungry grasp, depending on your
preference to live or die. Either way you have a
say. It's not love if it has to tell you

to move. It's not love if you leave in the
middle of the ocean. It's not love if you decide
to feed the tigers your favorite moon in order to
make a quick getaway. The world isn't quite working. The
weeds are only trying to make
it to Nirvana. You can't blame them. Yet
the collective mob want to blame everything on God. It's
not God if you don't recognize your own deepest feeling.
You don't need angels to tell
you if you are thirsty. The world hasn't ended. Your part
in it is as unique as a
snowflake butterfly riding on a hummingbird's
fuzzy back.
So for them to say God is dead
because they have more guns than anyone else aimed at
the back of your head is a lie.
It's a lie to believe that new people have nothing new to
offer. They always have themselves. And that's the song of
this poem. I'm inventing it right now. It doesn't have to
look like all
the other poems. It doesn't have to work the same way
twice. It doesn't have to end like this. You could give it an
altogether different name and
place. The world's alive. Your part in it is yours
to claim. You see poets do it all the time.

Damaged UFO

Came to a full stop. This is
a jarring realization to a pilot as
you can imagine. Flying by the seat
of your pants is not really an
option. It's over pretty quickly. I could
see through the slits for my eyes
you were already walking your way home

without me. This hurt more than a
broken heart. It would take some time
to get up and get out of
there before your men in their white
uniforms showed up. You hear the pocketful
of keys first, like a rattlesnake under
a wooden stoop, then the helicopter blades,

then the cocking of rifles. Better to
disappear than be snagged by one of
your so-called friends for examination or
experimentation.
I limped off as best as I
could, but the broken heart wouldn't stop
buzzing inside my chest. Still somehow I
made it away from the crash site

without being detected. My ship was ruined
beyond repair, but something of me lived,
wished to smile again, in spite of
the incredible pain. That's all I can
manage here. There is no magic or
science involved. It's been a day by
day operation. Here's that kiss I borrowed.

A Darryl Note About Poetry

Poetry should always be something you invent on purpose, not something you learn how to copy because you are good at following rules, if you ask me. Poetry is something you define inside the independent action of just doing it, not something that is defined by the poetic doings of a string of others, no matter how well-meaning or serious or intellectual or philosophical they may be about it, because it is a free choice you make in the process of your being creative with words, with sounds and meanings, with feelings and neuroses if you like, whatever moves you to express yourself. It is not a narrow state of being or mind, nor is it a completely solid thing like mud, heavy and ponderous, but it should be infinitely fluid like the morning sky, mysterious like the ocean, full of its own stars and planets, like a deep breath taken on purpose. Poetry is a partnership with your own deepest feelings. It's not a silly chess game with the reader. It's a gift that only happens when you are honest enough to let it speak on its own behalf. Poetry is a certain kind of music, the kind that asks you to listen, and when you do, rewards you with an incredible sound only you can hear and act upon because it is alive within you. Poetry lets you see, magnifies the truth and beauty of the poetry in everything around you. But it can't do it alone. It needs you. Your thoughts, your emotions, your dreams, your smiles, your tears, your desires, your words.

Just because someone has written a wonderful book about the meaning of poetry does not mean that you have to stop thinking about or looking for the meaning for yourself. Just because someone has earned a learned degree or written another bestselling book or won another prestigious award for their kind of poetry does not mean that they can speak for you. Just because you like someone's poetry doesn't mean you owe them anything. It's more than okay to disagree with anyone's thoughts about the true nature of poetry—even those who have been judged masters—because real, true poetry is not something that is dead and gone, but something with the very real possibility of being right here right now at all times and in all places. Everyone has the inalienable right to make their own poetry out of their own heads. It is not just for the academically rich and never was. That's just a damned lie dreamed up by some nasty people a long time ago to control the world. All these people with their many hard and fast rules for poetry are just trying to fix the game and own it and keep it away from those they despise for being different. Poetry rules are usually for those with cruel and petty minds. No house rules are for those with pretty-enough minds who just might express themselves in surprising and interesting ways if given half the chance. So first of all poetry has to be set free by the poets in all of us. Otherwise it isn't poetry at all but just some bright new monstrously gilded imitation hanging on a brightly lit painted wall.

Finally poetry is like love. You can't contain it, but if you are lucky you can only try to find a graceful way to be in its presence without making a complete and utter fool of yourself. And like love, it won't be smothered or it will simply disappear from view like it never happened and become something else, something less desirable and more sinister. It's a direct question of striking the right balance between self-expression and art. Poetry shines a proper light, but that doesn't mean it can't be misused by the enemy to blind or redirect an incoming good energy, so that brings me to my last point. Poetry is a responsibility. It's not for the faint of heart. It asks a lot, even of those it need not. It wants your full attention, your full devotion, but it promises you nothing in return but the sensation of the moment. You must take it on faith—faith that someone else out there can or will relate to its form and function, faith that you are doing the job of outlining it in your own words quite well, faith that you are not boring the shit out of the very leaves on the very trees, faith that you can get the body on the slab to get up and walk, maybe even to dance.

Acknowledgements

I'm not going to present you with a list of names. Instead I'm going to give you a list of actions. Thank you to those who make us laugh. Thank you to those whose hearts are big enough for mercy. Thank you to those who are brave enough to let every action, every thought, be an act of love towards all beings. Thank you to those who often save us and heal us through their daily expressions of loving kindness. Thank you to those who explore, who invent, who teach, who express universal emotions through the arts, who imagine, who work and play and raise families. Thank you to those remarkable persons who fall in love and stay in love. And, finally, thank you to those whose goodwill outlives us all.

An About the Author by the Author

Even though Darryl Price considers himself primarily a nature poet, he has three main people influences in his work and his art to thank.

The first is Emily Dickinson, who liked to lower a basket full of goodies on a string down from her window to the neighborhood children while hiding herself away from the rest of the world in her room all her life. She was louder than you might think, but you need a certain ocean shell to hear her laughing. It's a beautiful, mischievous shared mirth.

The second is John Lennon, the traumatized young Liverpool musician who changed the world with his unique genius and quick wit for storytelling through making real and timeless folk art out of rock and roll with his Beatle bandmates.

The third is Patti Smith, the amazing punk pioneer and best-selling author, photographer and poetess who set the world on fire with Horses, her brilliant and beautiful first album.

Emily believed in Emily the poet long before the world ever did. She insisted that the poetry she wrote be hers alone to invent. She invented Emily Dickinson's brand of poetry all by herself. She guarded it with her life. It came to her begging for attention on scraps of paper, paper bags and even corners of envelopes as well as note cards and letter stationary. It was kept always because it had value always in Emily's heart and mind. She was ahead of the curve of her time and this cost her dearly in terms of loneliness and self-imposed isolation. Still she is regarded as one of the main forces behind the birth of modern poetry along with Walt Whitman and a few others and remains one of the most beloved figures in all of American literature. She was the first poet Darryl Price ever invested in emotionally, reading everything by her and about her that he could get his hands on. His quest for her spiritual companionship continues to this day.

John Lennon was broken as a child by his free-spirited mother and his wayward seafaring father. They bounced him between them once too often for his own good and put a good-sized chip on his shoulder for life. But Aunt Mimi and Uncle George stepped in and showed the boy some actual love and concern, but the damage had already been done. Then Uncle George died. Then his mom was run over by a car. Then his best friend, Stuart, died and John felt more alone than ever. When he met his soon to be writing partner, Paul McCartney, they bonded over the fact that both their mothers had died. This didn't stop the two boys from dreaming big, maybe the biggest postwar dreams any young English kids could ever think of—to be bigger than Elvis! They sweated it out in dirty cellars and neon-infused nightclubs while learning their stock and trade as musicians. In the beginning it was all about the beats, but as they grew up and out, John became more concerned with his lyrics being seen and heard as real poetry. This added depth to their already beautiful sounds until it became the soundtrack for the whole world's turning for a brief moment in time. It inspired everything everywhere with a new renewed sense of wonder and joyous cause for celebration. It certainly inspired Darryl Price to be a more aware person who writes poetry on the planet. John's music is still a sacred touchstone for comfort and courage to him and countless others all across the universe.

Patti Smith is a hero in all senses of the word to Darryl Price. She represents to him the proof that the world needs to hear that poetry is alive and well in the human condition and always will be. Patti Smith makes it clear that the poetry of our lives is the poetry of all lives past, present and future. She is a singular, remarkable voice that lifts the spirits of all who witness it in concert, in film and in books. She snarls, she prays, she pronounces the love that is her poetry like the most precious gift one can give. She exemplifies courage and conviction, vulnerability and genuine affection, and still resoundingly entertains, entices and embraces her audiences with deeply-felt humanity and wit and charm. Darryl Price is a fan and proud of it, glad of it because she is the consummate poet of our time and for our time, making us incredibly lucky to be alive.

I would love to hear from you. Please contact me at **dprice1565@gmail.com** or in care of my publisher, Bud Smith. Thanks so very much for being a part of the journey of this book. It's very much appreciated. dp

www.ingramcontent.com/pod-product-compliance
Lightning Source LLC
Chambersburg PA
CBHW051731040426
42447CB00008B/1084